FOCUS

on Grammar and Punctuation

Grammar and Punctuation

Book 4

Louis Fidge

Collins

FOCUS

on Grammar
and Punctuation

Using this book

This book will help you to understand grammar and punctuation, and improve your writing. You will learn how sentences are structured and formed, how words work together and the rules of our language. Punctuation goes hand in hand with grammar – punctuation marks make writing easier to understand.

What's in a unit

Each unit is set out in the same way as the example here. There are also Progress Units to help you check how well you are doing.

Unit heading
This tells you what you will be learning about

The rule
This explains the rule and gives an example

Making sure
Activities to practise and develop your understanding

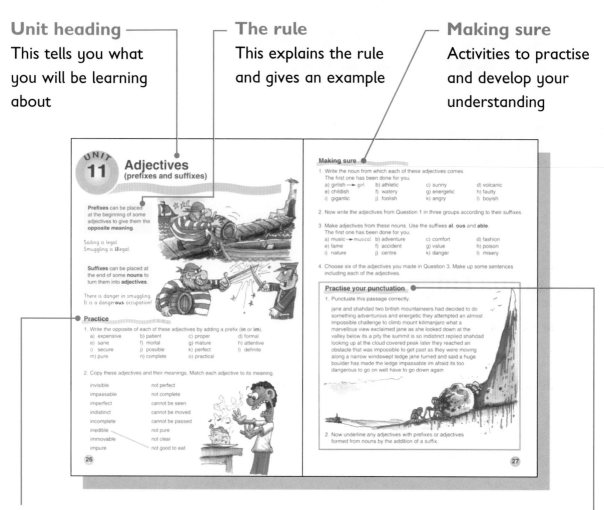

Practice
Activities to practise and check your understanding

Practise your punctuation
Activities to practise and check your punctuation

Contents

Parts of Speech
(nouns, adjectives, verbs, adverbs, pronouns and prepositions)

Grammar is the study of the way in which we use words to make **sentences**. Words may be divided into groups called **parts of speech** (or word classes). Six important **parts of speech** are: **nouns**, **adjectives**, **verbs**, **adverbs**, **pronouns** and **prepositions**.

This is a **pronoun**.
It stands **in place of a noun**.

This is an **adjective**.
It is a **describing** word.
It **tells us more about a noun**.

This is a **noun**.
It is a **naming word**.

He looked carefully at the **elastic** bandage **around** Amy's **knee**.

This is a **verb**.
It is a word that describes **actions**.

This is an adverb.
It **tells us more about the verb**.

This is a **preposition**.
It tells us the **position** of one thing **in relation to another**.

Practice

1. Copy these sentences. Underline the verbs in red, the adverbs in blue and the prepositions in green.
   a) Jamal carefully placed the heavy case on the bed.
   b) Slowly the tortoise plodded under the hedge.
   c) Jemma looked at the floor and apologised tearfully to her teacher.
   d) Yesterday the girls went into town.

2. Copy these sentences. Underline the nouns in blue, the adjectives in green and the pronouns in red.
   a) I tripped over the loose floorboard.
   b) Will she buy the most expensive dress?
   c) When the old man reached the bench, he sat down.
   d) Cartoons are popular because they make us laugh.

Making sure

Make up six silly sentences using words from the sacks. Do it like this:

Yesterday a spotty dinosaur from Leeds suddenly attacked me.

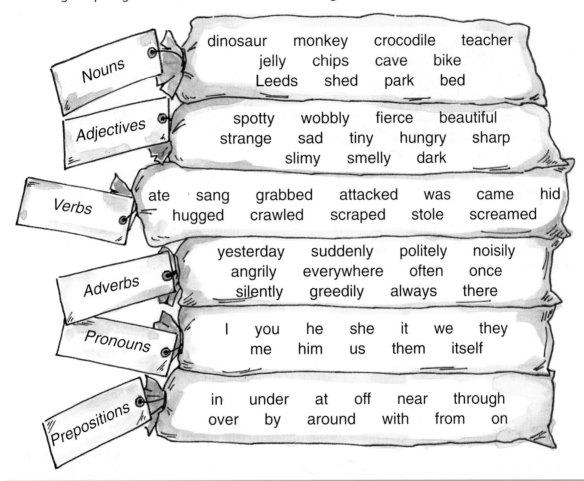

Nouns

dinosaur   monkey   crocodile   teacher
jelly   chips   cave   bike
Leeds   shed   park   bed

Adjectives

spotty   wobbly   fierce   beautiful
strange   sad   tiny   hungry   sharp
slimy   smelly   dark

Verbs

ate   sang   grabbed   attacked   was   came   hid
hugged   crawled   scraped   stole   screamed

Adverbs

yesterday   suddenly   politely   noisily
angrily   everywhere   often   once
silently   greedily   always   there

Pronouns

I   you   he   she   it   we   they
me   him   us   them   itself

Prepositions

in   under   at   off   near   through
over   by   around   with   from   on

Practise your punctuation

1. Rewrite this limerick. Punctuate it correctly.

   there was a young man from darjeeling
   who travelled by bus into ealing
   a man near the door
   said dont sit on the floor
   so he carefully sat on the ceiling

2. How many of the following can you find in the limerick?
   a) nouns   b) adjectives   c) verbs
   d) adverbs e) pronouns   f) prepositions
   Write them in your book.

Verbs
(regular and irregular)

Anna **looks** at the cake. (**present tense**)
Anna **looked** at the cake. (**past tense**)

She **eats** a piece. (**present tense**)
She **ate** a piece. (**past tense**)

Some **verbs** are **regular**.
This means that the main part of
the verb (the **root**) stays the
same when the tense changes.

Some **verbs** are **irregular**.
This means that the **root** of
the verb changes when the
tense changes.

Practice

1. Put each of these verbs into the past tense.

a) is	b) call	c) blow	d) walk	e) wash
f) catch	g) open	h) feel	i) miss	j) invite
k) find	l) bring	m)cook	n) help	o) write

2. Write **r** after each regular verb and **i** after each irregular verb.

3. Put each of these sentences into the past tense.
   The first one has been done for you.
   a) The driver makes a mistake. *The driver made a mistake.*
   b) The waiter pours a drink.
   c) We give the cat some milk.
   d) You drink a bottle of pop.
   e) I fall over and break my leg.
   f) The actor performs well.
   g) She celebrates her birthday.
   h) My mum bakes some lovely cakes.
   i) The child shakes with cold.

4. Now underline the verbs in the sentences you have written.
   Write **r** above each regular verb and **i** above each irregular verb.

Making sure

We can write verbs in the simple past tense or in the past tense using has or have.

Copy and complete this chart.

Present tense	Simple past tense	Past tense using **has** or **have**	Regular (**r**) or irregular (**i**)
I drink	I drank	I have drunk	i
I speak	I spoke		i
I collect		I have collected	r
I skate	I skated		
	I took		
		I have done	i
I nibble			
I steal	I stole		
		I have known	
	I froze	I have frozen	

Practise your punctuation

1. Punctuate these sentences correctly. Write the correct form of each underlined verb.
   a) when will <u>throwed</u> the stick fido his pet dog <u>bringed</u> it back again
   b) please miss I have <u>broke</u> my pencil jane <u>sayed</u>
   c) abdi <u>cryed</u> loudly someone has <u>took</u> my pencil
   d) on thursday bill <u>done</u> his work well and <u>writed</u> very neatly
   e) has paula <u>drawed</u> many good pictures
   f) beth <u>would have chose</u> a lolly but they <u>was</u> all sold

Verbs
(transitive; active and passive)

subject	verb
↓	↓
The Trojans	shouted.

subject	verb	object
↓	↓	↓
The Trojans	fought	the enemy.

Every **sentence** has a **subject** and a **verb**.

Some **sentences** also have an **object**. The **object** is the **person or thing affected by the verb**. **Verbs** which take an **object** are called **transitive verbs**.

The Trojans **defeated** the enemy.

The enemy **was defeated by** the Trojans.

A **verb** is **active** when the subject of the sentence does the action.

A **verb** is **passive** when the subject of the sentence has the action done to it.

Practice

Match each subject with a transitive verb and an object.
The first one has been done for you.

The Romans invaded Britain.

	Subjects	Verbs	Objects
1.	The Romans	eat	long dresses.
2.	Queen Victoria	invaded	his field.
3.	The angry bull	married	the ball.
4.	Farmer Giles	hit	nuts.
5.	The young princess	chased	Britain.
6.	Squirrels	wore	the boy.
7.	The tennis player	ploughed	a foreign prince.

Making sure

1. Rewrite these sentences. Change the verb
   from the active to the passive in each one.
   The first one has been done for you.
   a) Mighty walls surrounded the city.
      The city was surrounded by mighty walls.
   b) Mr Azadi won first prize in the raffle.
   c) St George killed the dragon.
   d) The helicopter rescued the stranded mountaineer.
   e) The officer in charge devised a clever plan.
   f) Some fierce pirates boarded the merchant ship.
   g) Amy switched on the computer.
   h) The shop assistant picked up the telephone.

2. Now rewrite these sentences.
   Change the verb from the passive to the
   active in each one.
   a) Mrs Baker was examined by the doctor.
   b) The city gates were opened by the soldiers.
   c) The squirrels were chased by the neighbour's ginger cat.
   d) The small boy was bullied by a group of older children.
   e) The princess was locked in the tower by Rumpelstiltskin.
   f) The washing was hung out to dry by Mr Fensome.
   g) A new song was performed by the pop star.
   h) The white stallion was ridden by Emperor Caligula.

Practise your punctuation

1. Punctuate these sentences correctly.
   a) the president of the united states
      summoned his advisers
   b) the gold medal was won by china
   c) roald dahl wrote many childrens books
   d) the jagged rock tore pedros shirt
   e) the chocolates sweets crisps and cakes
      were eaten by the hungry children
   f) smudge my pet dog ate the big juicy bone

2. In each sentence:
   a) underline the subject
   b) circle the verb

Adverbs

An **adverb** is a word which gives **more meaning** to a **verb**.

The fish moved its fins **gently**.

Then it blew some bubbles.

It swam **upwards** to the surface.

An **adverb of manner** tells us **how** something happened.

An **adverb of time** tells us **when** something happened.

An **adverb of place** tells us **where** something happened.

Practice

1. Write the opposite of each of these adverbs of manner.
   a) gently   b) quietly   c) happily   d) jerkily   e) carefully

2 Write the opposite of each of these adverbs of time.
   a) lastly   b) afterwards   c) tomorrow   d) earlier   e) now

3. Write the opposite of each of these adverbs of place.
   a) somewhere   b) inside   c) forwards   d) here   e) downwards

Making sure

Adverbs sometimes need an extra word to make their meaning more precise. Copy the sentences. Complete each sentence with a suitable adverb from the box.

rather heavily	really hard	so loudly	quite noisily	very badly
most often	almost always	much harder	more often	less well

1. Our teacher told us not to talk _____ _____.

2. The old lady fell _____ _____.

3. We tried _____ _____ to win the game.

4. Kylie _____ _____ chooses chips for tea.

5. After I was told off, I tried _____ _____ with my writing.

6. The thirsty dog drank the milk _____ _____.

7. Sara did her spellings _____ _____. She did _____ _____ than last week.

8. James smiles _____ _____ than I do but Kirsty smiles _____ _____.

Practise your punctuation

1. Punctuate these sentences correctly.
   a) lions seldom drink at the same place twice
   b) slow down dont walk so quickly grumbled old mr saunders
   c) donna waited very patiently in the queue for the singers autograph
   d) youve done quite well mark exclaimed mrs francis however I think you can try even harder
   e) after the explosion the house collapsed very quickly
   f) the stamp collector said you very rarely see a stamp from iceland today

2. Now underline all the adverbs in the sentences you have written.

Phrases
(adjective and adverb)

Sometimes we need to use a **phrase** instead of an **adjective** or an **adverb**.

The snow, **smooth, clean and white,** looks good enough to eat.

Mrs Squires is watching the children playing **in the snow**.

This phrase tells us more about the noun **snow**. It is an **adjective phrase**.

This phrase tells us more about the verb **playing**. It is an **adverb phrase**.

Practice

1. Choose the most suitable adjective phrase to complete each of the sentences.

> long and white   cold and draughty   taller than a house
> full of shopping   with its high, grey walls

a) The lady was carrying a bag, _____.
b) _____, the old man's beard nearly reached the floor.
c) The castle, _____ , looked rather frightening.
d) The large room was _____.
e) The giant, _____ , stamped his foot angrily.

2. Choose the most suitable adverb phrase to complete each of the sentences.

> quietly and attentively   as quick as a flash   after tea
> carelessly and untidily   on the school field

a) They went home _____.
b) We played rounders _____.
c) We sat, _____ , listening to the story.
d) The lion pounced, _____.
e) Raza wrote his story _____ .

Making sure

1. Copy these sentences. Underline the adjective phrase in each one.
   a) The sheep, glad to be out of doors, were grazing in the field.
   b) The apples, fresh and crisp, were from New Zealand.
   c) The boy stopped suddenly, filled with fear.
   d) Heavy and solid, the door creaked noisily as we pushed it open.
   e) We chose the chair with the comfortable cushions.

2. Now rewrite each sentence as two sentences.
   The first one has been done for you.
   a) The sheep were grazing in the field. They were glad to be out of doors.

3. Copy these sentences. Underline the adverb phrase in each one.
   Describe whether the phrase tells you how, where or when the
   action happened. The first one has been done for you.
   a) Every Friday we buy fish and chips. (when)
   b) Tim coloured the picture as carefully as possible.
   c) With a great effort, Mrs Lacey lifted the heavy case.
   d) The bird flew slowly but gracefully on to the top branch of the tree.
   e) The lion disappeared, merging into the background.

Practise your punctuation

1. Punctuate these pairs of sentences correctly.
   a) the farmer looked up at the sky it was cloudy and overcast
   b) harrys jeans were new and fashionable they came from
      the united states
   c) they crept through the forest they moved stealthily and quietly
   d) janes sister held her hand to cross the road her sister was
      older and more sensible

2. Now rewrite each pair of sentences as one sentence.
   Underline either an adverb phrase or an adjective phrase
   in each sentence. The first one has been done for you.
   a) The farmer looked up at the cloudy and overcast sky. (adjective phrase)

UNIT 6

Nouns
(singular and plural)

Most **nouns** may be written in either the **singular (one)** or the **plural (more than one)**.
Most **nouns** follow **rules** for making the **plural** form.

| one tree | one leaf | one bush | one daisy |

| two tree**s** | two lea**ves** | two bush**es** | two dais**ies** |

| Most nouns just add **s**. | Most nouns ending in **f** or **fe** take **ves**. | Nouns ending in **sh**, **ch**, **s** or **x** add **es**. | Nouns ending in a consonant + **y** take **ies**. |

Practice

1. Write the plural form of each of these nouns.
   a) emperor   b) skill   c) life   d) body   e) ash
   f) wife   g) watch   h) dish   i) country   j) loaf
   k) wolf   l) fly

2. Write the singular form of each of these nouns.
   a) cities   b) seeds   c) monkeys   d) shelves   e) thieves
   f) foxes   g) brothers   h) impurities   i) wishes   j) dresses
   k) halves   l) factories

3. Rewrite the following sentences. Change each singular noun into a plural noun. Make any other necessary changes. The first one has been done for you.
   a) The poppy is a lovely flower.
      Poppies are lovely flowers.
   b) The boy wrote in the diary.
   c) The fox hid in the bush.
   d) The lady put the loaf on the shelf.
   e) The girl played with the baby and then tried on the dress.

The subject of the sentence and the verb should always agree.

Making sure

1. Some plurals do not follow the rules. Write the plural form of each of these singular nouns. The first two have been done for you.

   a) ox ➤ oxen   b) fish ➤ fish   c) deer   d) foot   e) goose

   f) mouse   g) sheep   h) man   i) child

2. Copy this chart. Write each of the singular nouns from Question 1 in the correct column.

Nouns which change in unexpected ways in the plural	Nouns which don't change at all in the plural

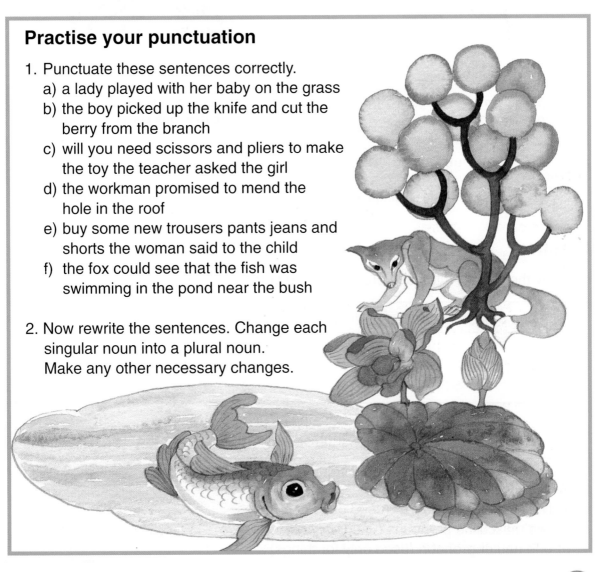

Practise your punctuation

1. Punctuate these sentences correctly.
   a) a lady played with her baby on the grass
   b) the boy picked up the knife and cut the berry from the branch
   c) will you need scissors and pliers to make the toy the teacher asked the girl
   d) the workman promised to mend the hole in the roof
   e) buy some new trousers pants jeans and shorts the woman said to the child
   f) the fox could see that the fish was swimming in the pond near the bush

2. Now rewrite the sentences. Change each singular noun into a plural noun. Make any other necessary changes.

Pronouns

Sometimes when we are talking about people or things we use **pronouns** instead of **nouns**.

me

us

Pronouns may be **singular** (**one** person or thing).

Pronouns may be **plural** (**more than one** person or thing).

you

The pronoun **you** may be **singular**.

you

The pronoun **you** may be **plural**.

Practice

1. Copy the chart. Write each pronoun in the correct column.

Singular pronouns	Plural pronouns
I	we

I	he	you	they	us	me	she
it	you	them	we	him	her	

2. Write down:
   a) two feminine pronouns (used only for females)
   b) two masculine pronouns (used only for males)
   c) one neuter pronoun (used only for things)

Making sure

Copy the chart. Write each pronoun in the correct box.

me	mine	yourselves	yourself	him	she	hers
it	ourselves	us	ours	them	themselves	theirs

	Singular pronouns	Plural pronouns
First person (about **me**)	I	we
Second person (about **you**)	you	you
Third person (about **someone** or **something else**)	he	they

Practise your punctuation

1. Punctuate these sentences correctly.
    a) i suppose you think youre funny the teacher said to emma
    b) stop spoiling our game leave us alone fatima and chloe shouted at darren
    c) is this your pen mrs harris asked yes i think it is mine replied mustafa
    d) chandrika and carra were being teased by two big boys they were calling them names

2. Now underline all the pronouns in the sentences you have written.

Capital Letters

There are various uses for **capital letters**, apart from **beginning sentences**, **beginning new lines in a poem** and using the pronoun **I**.

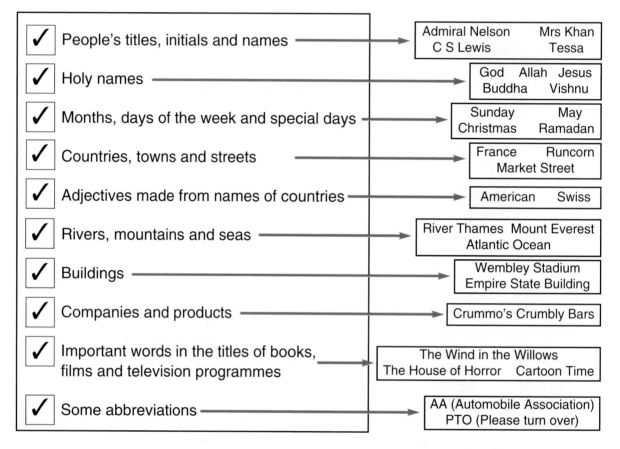

✓	People's titles, initials and names	→	Admiral Nelson Mrs Khan C S Lewis Tessa
✓	Holy names	→	God Allah Jesus Buddha Vishnu
✓	Months, days of the week and special days	→	Sunday May Christmas Ramadan
✓	Countries, towns and streets	→	France Runcorn Market Street
✓	Adjectives made from names of countries	→	American Swiss
✓	Rivers, mountains and seas	→	River Thames Mount Everest Atlantic Ocean
✓	Buildings	→	Wembley Stadium Empire State Building
✓	Companies and products	→	Crummo's Crumbly Bars
✓	Important words in the titles of books, films and television programmes	→	The Wind in the Willows The House of Horror Cartoon Time
✓	Some abbreviations	→	AA (Automobile Association) PTO (Please turn over)

Practice

Copy this list of words. Put in capital letters where necessary.

1. mountain
2. tuesday
3. tower bridge
4. sweden
5. month
6. british gas
7. humpty dumpty
8. dutch
9. kent
10. measles
11. bristol
12. film
13. saint peter
14. city
15. the mississippi
16. george street
17. queen mary
18. easter

Making sure

1. Punctuate these book titles correctly.
   a) the lion the witch and the wardrobe
   b) black beauty
   c) treasure island
   d) charlie and the chocolate factory
   e) gullivers travels
   f) the wizard of oz

2. Copy and correct this extract from a television guide.

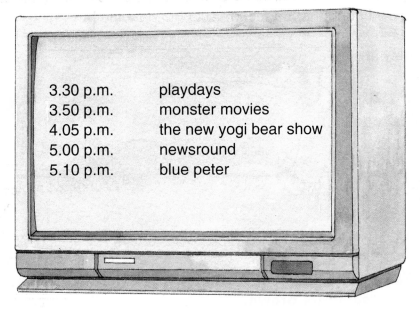

3.30 p.m.	playdays
3.50 p.m.	monster movies
4.05 p.m.	the new yogi bear show
5.00 p.m.	newsround
5.10 p.m.	blue peter

3. Write the abbreviation for each of these.
   The first one has been done for you.
   a) Member of Parliament   MP
   b) On Her Majesty's Service
   c) Prime Minister
   d) United States of America
   e) British Broadcasting Corporation
   f) Her Majesty's Ship

Practise your punctuation

Punctuate these sentences correctly.

1. the houses of parliament are near big ben in london

2. uncle daves birthday is on 8th november

3. argentina brazil colombia and peru are countries in south america

4. last july i visited italy on holiday i stayed at the dolce vita hotel

5. mr and mrs broom went to see the film called the lost ark at the odeon cinema in leeds

6. ben nevis is a mountain in scotland

Direct Speech

When we write down someone's **exact** words, we call it **direct speech**.
We use **inverted commas** (**speech marks**) to mark the beginning
and end of what the person says. Whenever a **new person** starts speaking,
we start a **new line**.

This could be written down in three different ways using **direct speech**. Notice the **punctuation** in each.

Your father has gone away for a few days, so I hope you'll be good.

Pattern 1   **Mrs Brown said, "Your father has gone away for a few days, so I hope you'll be good."**

Pattern 2   **"Your father has gone away for a few days, so I hope you'll be good,"said Mrs Brown.**

Pattern 3   **"Your father has gone away for a few days," said Mrs Brown, "so I hope you'll be good."**

Practice

1. Rewrite this conversation using Pattern 2.

Peter asked, "Is something the matter?"
Mrs Brown replied, "Don't worry. Everything is fine."
Roberta said," I hope Dad won't be away too long."
Mrs Brown answered, "He should be back soon."

2. Rewrite this conversation using Pattern 1.

"It's time for bed," Mrs Brown said to the children.
"Can't we stay up a bit longer?" Peter begged.
"I'm afraid it's already past your bedtime," Mrs Brown
replied with a smile.
"Goodnight, Mum. I'll see you in the morning,"
Roberta called as she went upstairs.

Making sure

Punctuate this passage with inverted commas.
Remember to start a new line each time a new person starts to speak.

I'm afraid I've had some bad news, Mrs Brown said to the children. Your father has had an accident. What's the matter? Roberta asked. Is it serious? Will he have to go to hospital? Peter asked. Will he have to have an operation? Now don't worry, Mrs Brown replied. It's not as bad as that. Someone crashed into his car but he hasn't broken any bones. That's a relief! Roberta exclaimed. But I bet he's a bit shaken up! He sounded fine on the telephone, Mrs Brown said, but the car is badly damaged. A damaged car, said Peter, is better than a damaged Dad!

Practise your punctuation

1. Punctuate this passage. It is written in indirect speech, so inverted commas are not needed.

mr brown asked the salesman how much the new car was the salesman asked mr brown whether he had an old car to trade in mr brown replied that he had just had an accident and that his car had been badly damaged the salesman told him that it didnt matter as he was sure that they could agree on a good price mr brown asked if he could go for a test run in the new car to try it out the salesman agreed but told him to take care because one smashed car was enough

2. Now rewrite the passage, setting it out like a play. Start it like this:

Mr Brown: How much is that new car?
Salesman: Have you got an old car to trade in?

Nouns (concrete and abstract)

Concrete nouns are the names of **things which exist outside your mind**.
You can touch, taste, see, hear or smell these things.

Abstract nouns are nouns which represent **thoughts, ideas and feelings**.
You cannot touch, taste, see, hear or smell these things.

I tried to stand, but found, to my **astonishment**, that I could not move. I was tied up with **rope**.

This is an **abstract noun**.

This is a **concrete noun**.

Practice

1. Copy this chart and write each noun in the correct column.

bread	honesty	caravan	pen	emptiness	wonder
	door	beauty	computer	belief	

Concrete nouns	Abstract nouns

2. Copy the sentences. Complete each one with an abstract noun from the box.

danger	fear	speed	poverty	strength	anger

a) The giant had the _____ of ten men.

b) The little people were terrified and looked at the giant with _____.

c) The _____ of the car was amazing.

d) There is _____ in climbing mountains.

e) The cook was filled with _____ when she saw the mess in the kitchen.

f) The beggar lived in _____.

Making sure

1. Copy these sentences. Underline the abstract noun in each sentence.
   a) The old man had great patience.
   b) There was love in the eyes of the mother when she held her new baby.
   c) Louise looked at her present in astonishment.
   d) The beauty of the mountains was incredible.
   e) If you could have one wish, what would it be?
   f) The explorer showed courage when she was attacked by a wild bear.

2. Change each of these adjectives into an abstract noun.
   The first one has been done for you.
   a) sick ⟶ sickness

b) ugly	c) dark	d) dangerous
e) hot	f) joyful	g) foolish
h) silly	i) high	j) wealthy

3. Now make up five sentences containing some of the
   abstract nouns you have made.

Practise your punctuation

1. Punctuate these sentences correctly.
   a) when mrs grant confronted the thief she saw fear in his eyes
   b) the judge who had a long white beard praised the witness
      for her honesty
   c) the funfair caused great excitement when it came to bradford
   d) mr younnas was filled with happiness when he won the lottery
   e) blinking and stumbling i was blinded by the brightness of the torch
   f) my grandad used to spend hours playing with me i was amazed
      at his patience

2. Now underline the nouns in each sentence. Write:
   a) **c** above each concrete noun
   b) **a** above each abstract noun

Progress Test A

1. Write each of these verbs in the past tense.
   Write **r** after each **regular verb**, and **i** after each **irregular verb**.
   a) find   b) wonder   c) drink   d) see   e) refuse
   f) decide   g) take   h) hug   i) defeat   j) teach

2. Copy these sentences. Choose the correct form of the verb to complete each one.
   a) I have _____ in a helicopter. (fly)
   b) The workers have _____ a big house. (build)
   c) The spectators have all _____ the stadium. (leave)
   d) If I had _____ louder they would have _____ me. (shout, hear)
   e) The baby had only just _____ up. (wake)

3. Copy the chart. Put each of the words in the box in the correct column.

Parts of speech					
Nouns	Adjectives	Verbs	Adverbs	Pronouns	Prepositions

car   ran   he   in   slowly   huge   quietly   they   under   house
cold   ate   telephone   looked   us   behind   empty   greedily

4. Each of these sentences contains a **transitive verb**. Copy the sentences, writing **s** above each subject, **v** above each verb and **o** above each object.
   a) The cricketer preferred his new bat.
   b) The famous opera singer sang a lovely song.
   c) The ball broke the window.
   d) The old man peeled the rosy, red apple.
   e) The old lady knitted a woolly jumper.

5. Now rewrite the sentences in Question 4, changing the verbs from the **active** to the **passive**.

6. Copy these adverbs. Write **m** after each **adverb of manner**, **t** after each **adverb of time**, and **p** after each **adverb of place**.
   a) wearily   b) upwards   c) later   d) before   e) cautiously
   f) there   g) narrowly   h) yesterday   i) backwards j) loudly

7. Make up some sentences including these adverbs.
   a) so badly   b) very smartly   c) fairly often   d) rather quietly

8. Copy the sentence below. Underline the **adjective phrase** in it.
   Circle the **adverb phrase**.

   The hot and sticky baby played in the bath.

9. Write the **plural** of each of these nouns:
   a) half   b) church   c) city   d) fly   e) mouse
   f) rat   g) dress   h) sheep   i) knife   j) child
   k) calf   l) box

10. Copy these words. Put in **capital letters** where necessary.
    a) france   b) snow white   c) title   d) jesus
    e) oxford street   f) american   g) computer   h) canterbury
    i) mars   j) big ben

11. Copy the chart. Write each of the **nouns** in the correct column.

Concrete nouns	Abstract nouns

   truth   lamp   potato   justice   speed   grass   bird   courage   shoe

12. Copy this passage and underline the **pronouns**.
    Write **s** above each singular pronoun and **p** above each plural pronoun.

    Emma and I climbed the tree. We saw a squirrel.
    It ran along the branch and joined some other squirrels.
    They took no notice of us. Emma slipped. She grabbed
    the branch tightly.
    "You had a narrow escape," I laughed.

25

UNIT 11

Adjectives
(prefixes and suffixes)

Prefixes can be placed at the beginning of some adjectives to give them the **opposite meaning**.

Sailing is legal.
Smuggling is **il**legal.

Suffixes can be placed at the end of some **nouns** to turn them into **adjectives**.

There is danger in smuggling. It is a danger**ous** occupation!

Practice

1. Write the opposite of each of these adjectives by adding a prefix (**in** or **im**).

a) expensive	b) patient	c) proper	d) formal
e) sane	f) mortal	g) mature	h) attentive
i) secure	j) possible	k) perfect	l) definite
m) pure	n) complete	o) practical	

2. Copy these adjectives and their meanings. Match each adjective to its meaning.

invisible   not perfect

impassable   not complete

imperfect   cannot be seen

indistinct   cannot be moved

incomplete   cannot be passed

inedible   not pure

immovable   not clear

impure   not good to eat

Making sure

1. Write the noun from which each of these adjectives comes.
   The first one has been done for you.
   a) girlish ➔ girl   b) athletic   c) sunny   d) volcanic
   e) childish   f) watery   g) energetic   h) faulty
   i) gigantic   j) foolish   k) angry   l) boyish

2. Now write the adjectives from Question 1 in three groups according to their suffixes.

3. Make adjectives from these nouns. Use the suffixes **al**, **ous** and **able**.
   The first one has been done for you.
   a) music ➔ musical   b) adventure   c) comfort   d) fashion
   e) fame   f) accident   g) value   h) poison
   i) nature   j) centre   k) danger   l) misery

4. Choose six of the adjectives you made in Question 3. Make up some sentences including each of the adjectives.

Practise your punctuation

1. Punctuate this passage correctly.

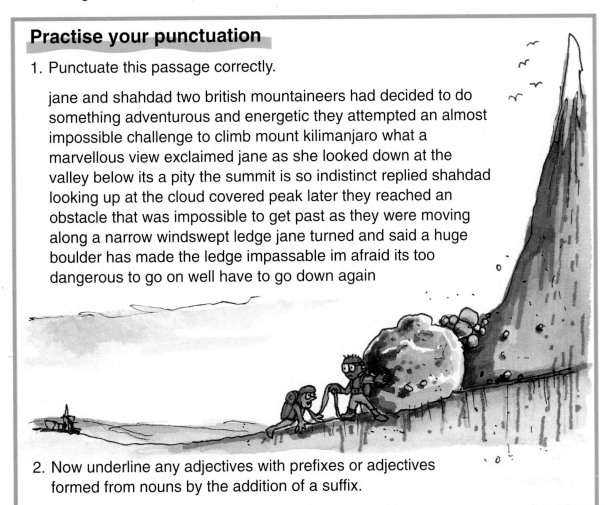

   jane and shahdad two british mountaineers had decided to do something adventurous and energetic they attempted an almost impossible challenge to climb mount kilimanjaro what a marvellous view exclaimed jane as she looked down at the valley below its a pity the summit is so indistinct replied shahdad looking up at the cloud covered peak later they reached an obstacle that was impossible to get past as they were moving along a narrow windswept ledge jane turned and said a huge boulder has made the ledge impassable im afraid its too dangerous to go on well have to go down again

2. Now underline any adjectives with prefixes or adjectives formed from nouns by the addition of a suffix.

UNIT 12 Clauses

A **clause** is a group of words which can be used either as a **whole sentence** or as **part of a sentence**. A **clause** always contains a **verb**.

The giant bent down.
He put his face close to Sophie's.

These are two **single-clause** sentences.

The giant bent down **and** put his face close to Sophie's.

We can make a **two-clause** sentence by joining the two **single-clause** sentences with a **conjunction**. (**Conjunctions** are sometimes called **connectives**.)

Practice

1. Use either the conjunction **and** or the conjunction **but** to join each of these pairs of single-clause sentences. The first one has been done for you.
   a) The giant looked frightening. He was friendly.
      The giant looked frightening but he was friendly.
   b) The giant walked up to Sophie. He put his case down.
   c) The case was small. It was very heavy.
   d) Sophie looked up at the giant. She smiled at him.
   e) It was a sunny day. Dark clouds were beginning to gather.

2. Copy these sentences. Underline the two clauses in each one.
   a) The giant jumped into the air and swung the net.
   b) He caught something in the net and laughed excitedly.
   c) Sophie picked up the jar and held it up for the giant.
   d) The giant tipped something into the jar and screwed on the lid.
   e) He held the jar close to his ear but heard nothing.

3. In the sentences you have written:
   a) write **v** above the verb in each clause
   b) circle the conjunction

Making sure

1. The more important clause in a two-clause sentence is called the main clause. The main clause is often a sentence in itself. Underline the main clause in each sentence.
   a) Sophie was friends with the giant although she was a little scared of him.
   b) The night was dark so it was difficult to see.
   c) I played with my friend after I had eaten my tea.
   d) The frog was irritating because it croaked so much.
   e) The kangaroo hopped away when the snake hissed at it.

2. Choose a conjunction from the box and add a second clause to each of these main clauses. The first one has been done for you.

so	although	because	after	before	when

   a) The disobedient boy sat down <u>before he had washed his hands</u>.
   b) The doctor examined the patient _____.
   c) The bird flew off _____.
   d) The hedgehog walked across the lawn _____.
   e) The children shivered in the cold wind _____.

Practise your punctuation

1. Punctuate these sentences correctly. Underline the main clause in each. (The main clause does not always come at the beginning of a sentence.)
   a) the odeon theatre was full because gary gold was so popular
   b) when gary came on to the stage the audience roared
   c) gary sang his latest song after a fan requested it
   d) although the band played loudly no one complained
   e) although he was tired gary put everything into his act
   f) gary signed autographs after the show had finished

2. Rewrite each sentence in a different way. The first one has been done for you.
   a) Because Gary Gold was so popular, the Odeon Theatre was full.

Complex Sentences

Every **sentence** contains at least
one main (most important) clause.
A **complex sentence** contains
one main clause and **one or more
subordinate (less important) clauses**.

The king was angry   when he saw the muddy footprints.

This is the **main clause**. It can be
used on its own as a sentence.

This is the **subordinate clause**.
It does not make sense on its own.

Practice

1. Match each main clause with a suitable subordinate clause.
   Write the complex sentences you make.

Main clauses	Subordinate clauses
Everyone started talking	although I watered them regularly.
Clouds form	where I saw the Pope.
The flowers did not grow	as soon as the teacher left the room.
The rabbit escaped	unless they are with their parents.
Children are not admitted	when water vapour in the air cools.
I visited Rome	because the hutch door was left open.

2. Make up a subordinate clause to finish each of these sentences.
   The first one has been done for you.
   a) It often rains in winter so <u>I always carry an umbrella</u>.
   b) The lollipop lady stopped the traffic until _____.
   c) We saw many elephants when _____.
   d) Mrs Kennedy won the Lottery so _____.
   e) You cannot have a sweet unless _____.
   f) The dog went to sleep after _____.

Making sure

1. Sometimes a subordinate clause is introduced by the pronoun **who** (when referring to a person) or the pronoun **which** (when referring to an animal or a thing). Copy and complete these sentences using either **who** or **which**. Underline the main clause and circle the subordinate clause in each sentence. The first two have been done for you.
   a) <u>I found the key</u> (_____which_____ opens the old box.)
   b) <u>Emma wrote to her uncle,</u> (_____who_____ had sent her a present.)
   c) Amir is the boy _____ won first prize.
   d) The police officer caught the thief, _____ had run away.
   e) I found the missing bag, _____ had been lost.

2. Choose the most suitable subordinate clause to complete each sentence.

> which had a hole in it   which was starving   who had stolen the money
>   which was singing loudly   who had hurt her toe

   a) The girl _____ was punished by her mother.
   b) The old boat, _____, sank in the lake.
   c) Emma, _____, was limping badly.
   d) The bird, _____, was a lark.
   e) The thin dog, _____, gobbled up all the food.

Practise your punctuation

1. Punctuate these sentences correctly.
   a) p c sharp arrested the man who had robbed the bank in runcorn road
   b) sharon bought a magazine which was full of pictures of her favourite band
   c) robin hood who was an outlaw lived in sherwood forest
   d) the man who invented television was called john logie baird
   e) mr cusack praised jamie who had tried very hard at english

2. Underline the main clause and circle the subordinate clause in each sentence.

Brackets and Hyphens

Brackets are **punctuation marks** which enclose information to show that it is **separate** from everything around it.

These are **brackets**.

The cars (shown above) looked like monsters with glowing eyes.

A **hyphen** is used when we join two words to make a **compound adjective**.

This is a **hyphen**.

The monster-like creature had long hair and glowing eyes.

Practice

1. Rewrite these sentences without brackets. Make each sentence into two sentences. The first one has been done for you.
   a) The puppies (rolling around the floor as usual) were playing when Mr Smith came in.
      The puppies were playing when Mr Smith came in. They were rolling around the floor as usual.
   b) Brackets (often used in a similar way to a pair of commas) are useful punctuation marks.
   c) Tower Bridge (which which opens up to let ships pass along the river) is quite an old bridge.
   d) Police officers (sometimes called "bobbies" or "peelers") get their nicknames from Sir Robert Peel.
   e) The shoes (made from the best leather) were very expensive.

2. Copy these sentences, putting in the missing brackets.
   a) The picture shown on page 7 is of an aeroplane landing.
   b) Commas like brackets are often used in pairs.
   c) You will find ants practically everywhere except on the summits of very high mountains.
   d) When a liquid evaporates changes into a gas it draws off heat
   e) If you eat a balanced diet you will get all the vitamins you need with the possible exception of Vitamin D.

Making sure

1. Find and write the compound adjectives in these sentences.
   a) The man shaved off his beard and became clean-shaven.
   b) The dog is house-trained. It never makes a mess.
   c) What is the difference between a man eating mammoth and
      a man-eating mammoth?
   d) My football-mad brother supports Liverpool.
   e) The sweet-tasting orange was from Spain.

2. Choose a word from the box to complete each compound adjective.

light	tongue	tight	animal	wide

   a) Someone who is mean is _____-fisted.
   b) Someone who steals is _____-fingered.
   c) Someone showing surprise may be _____-eyed.
   d) Someone who is nervous may be _____-tied.
   e) Someone who loves dogs is _____-loving.

Practise your punctuation

Punctuate these sentences.

1. ben sam's floppy eared dog was barking

2. the monster with the flashing blue green eyes ate
   anything it could find

3. do you know the way to norwich asked the
   stranger as he parked his car a blue
   hatchback

4. dont touch that button shouted the
   worried looking mother it might
   be dangerous

5. much of london including the
   original st pauls cathedral
   was destroyed in the
   great fire which
   happened in 1666

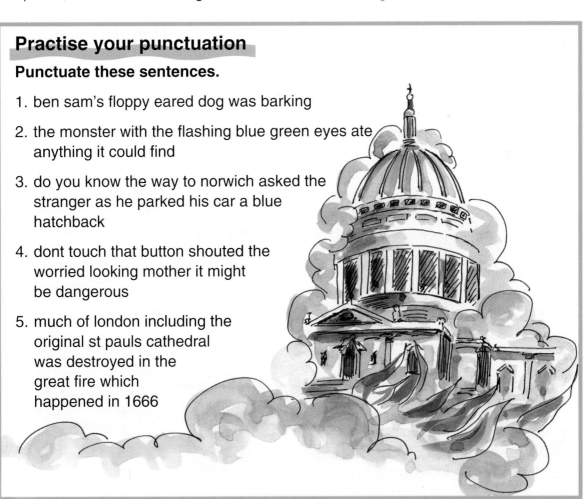

Paragraphs

A **paragraph** is a group of sentences that deals with **one main idea or topic**. A long piece of writing is easier to read if it is divided into paragraphs.

We open a new **paragraph** by beginning the first line a little way in from the margin. (This is called **indenting**.)

In ancient times, people bathed in water for two reasons: for cleanliness or for religious observance. The Romans liked to take warm baths to keep themselves clean. On the other hand, the Ancient Egyptians bathed chiefly for religious reasons.

Practice

These four paragraphs are jumbled up. Write them in the correct order.

In ancient times, the Greeks bathed in tubs made of polished stone. We know this because remains of such tubs have been found. Homer, a Greek poet, describes a beautiful silver tub in one of his poems.

By the Middle Ages, attitudes had changed. People rarely bathed at all. There were few private baths in homes. Many people used perfumes and cosmetics as a substitute for bathing to cover up any unpleasant smells.

Remains of the oldest known baths have been discovered on Crete. They are thought to be 4000 years old. There are footbaths and a very modern-looking tub.

It was not until Victorian times that bathrooms began to evolve as separate rooms in houses. The tub, made of wood, copper or iron, often had a cover over it to make it look like a sofa.

Making sure

1. Use these notes to write four paragraphs about the development of swimming.

Paragraph 1   Animals – natural swimmers – humans are not – had to learn – watched and imitated animals

Paragraph 2   Noticed how dogs swam – imitated "dog paddle" – developed breaststroke – co-ordinates arm and leg movements better

Paragraph 3   Next development – sidestroke – used scissors-kick – developed overarm stroke to accompany it – greater speed than breaststroke or dog paddle

Paragraph 4   1902 – Richard Cavill – introduced crawl from Australia – first called Australian crawl – fastest stroke – now most popular stroke

2. Imagine that you are a famous explorer. You want to reach the Temple of Tears, but first you have to pass through some dangerous country. Write a separate paragraph about each section of your journey.

The jungle   There are 25 miles of thick jungle to be cut through. Inhabiting the jungle are a variety of dangerous animals, as well as many poisonous insects.

The river   After this, you have to get across the wide, fast-flowing, muddy river. There is no bridge but there are many hungry crocodiles.

The mountain   The Temple is at the top of the mountain, which has steep, rocky sides, requiring ropes to climb them. Another problem is the danger of frequent landslides.

The Temple   Once you get to the Temple you still have to find a way in. Its walls are high and smooth, and its doors are heavy and impossible to open. There are no windows, but there is talk of invisible guardians who keep its secrets.

Practise your punctuation

Punctuate this passage correctly. Divide it into three separate paragraphs.

moles are found mainly in europe they spend most of their time underground digging complicated systems of tunnels and chambers the soil they dig up appears on the surface as molehills the appearance of moles is distinctive moles fur is soft like black velvet their front paws large and powerful are specially designed for digging their small eyes are nearly hidden by their fur in fact moles are virtually blind moles have an enormous appetite and seem to be constantly hungry the moles diet consists chiefly of earthworms a mole will eat up to its own weight of earthworms in a day they also eat larvae but will eat almost any animal matter

UNIT 16

Apostrophes
(contractions and possessive nouns)

There are two occasions when you should use an **apostrophe**:

- in a **contraction** (when two words are joined together and some letters are missed out)
- to show **ownership**

I'm going for a bike ride.

I'm is short for **I am**. The apostrophe shows that a letter is missing.

the **boy's** bike

the **girls'** skateboards

the **children's** skates

This means **the bike belonging to the boy**. When there is just one owner, we usually add **'s** to the noun.

This means **the skateboards belonging to the girls**. When there is more than one owner, we add **'** to the noun if it ends in **s**.

This means **the skates belonging to the children**. We add **'s** if there is no **s** at the end of the plural noun.

Practice

1. Write each of these contractions in full. The first one has been done for you.
   - a) I'm ➔ I am
   - b) I've
   - c) she's
   - d) you're
   - e) it's
   - f) haven't
   - g) couldn't
   - h) wasn't
   - i) aren't
   - j) who's
   - k) we're
   - l) let's
   - m) they've
   - n) she'll
   - o) we'd

2. Rewrite each of the sentences, using the shortened form of the underlined words.
   - a) I <u>had not</u> seen the film before.
   - b) He <u>did not</u> want it.
   - c) <u>That is</u> a good book.
   - d) <u>We will</u> help.
   - e) <u>You will</u> be sorry.
   - f) <u>Do not</u> go.
   - g) <u>It is</u> a good idea.
   - h) You <u>should not</u> come.
   - i) <u>They are</u> late.
   - j) It <u>would not</u> matter.
   - k) <u>We have</u> got two.
   - l) You <u>need not</u> go in.

Making sure

1. Write the possessive form of each of these singular nouns.
   The first one has been done for you.
   a) the hat of the clown  the clown's hat
   b) the antlers of the biggest deer
   c) the watch of the nurse
   d) the shell of the tortoise
   e) the tail of the tiger
   f) the claws of the cat
   g) the bike of my friend

2. Now write the possessive form of each of these plural nouns.
   a) the whiskers of the cats   b) the eggs of the birds
   c) the den of the wolves   d) the tools of the workmen
   e) the wool of the sheep   f) the club of the children
   g) the paws of the dogs   h) the manes of the lions
   i) the uniforms of the men

3. Copy these sentences. Complete each one with the possessive form of
   the noun in brackets.
   a) The _____ leg was broken in the crash. (motorist)
   b) The department store stocks lots of _____ clothes. (babies)
   c) Our _____ athletes always do well. (country)
   d) The _____ manes were well groomed. (horses)
   e) The _____ meeting took place after school. (teachers)
   f) We could not see the _____ flag. (ship)

Practise your punctuation

Punctuate these sentences correctly.

1. shanaz and ali who were playing in the park pulled
   a thorn out of the dogs paw

2. charles dickens a famous author wrote a book called
   oliver twist in which oliver became one of fagins thieves

3. dawns early light crept into the caves entrance allowing
   the explorers to see the paintings on the wall

4. my fathers job selling shoes takes him all over england

5. im going to take a photograph of the dinosaurs
   skeletons said the professor

Standard English

Standard English is the kind of language we use in writing.
It is used in education, government and business, and in most books.

Non-standard English is often used in everyday speech. We may say things differently from the way in which we would write them.

Non-standard English may differ from **Standard English** in two ways:
- **gramma**r (the way we form sentences)
- **vocabulary** (the words we use)

Buzz off, you kids!

In Standard English we would write this as: **Go away, you children.**

Practice

Write these sentences using Standard English vocabulary. The first one has been done for you.

1. Did you see that bloke with purple hair?

   Did you see that man with purple hair?

2. The old dear's got lots of moggies.

3. Button your lip and stop talking rubbish!

4. She's always stuffing her face, the greedy guts.

5. Shall we bunk off school today?

6. I spent five quid on the chocolates.

7. That's cool, man.

8. Tell me where you stashed the loot.

9. I think Chelsea are wicked!

10. I'll have bangers and mashed spuds for dinner, please.

Making sure

These sentences are grammatically incorrect. Write them again in Standard English. The first one has been done for you.

1. Me and Darren watched telly.
   Darren and I watched television.

2. Who's got me pen?

3. They coming soon.

4. He don't know nothing.

5. I aint got none.

6. We was just looking.

7. I don't want no trouble.

8. What you want?

9. I'm gonna get you.

10. That's the picture what I drew.

Practise your punctuation

1. Punctuate this passage, leaving it in non-standard English.

   carlo opened the door looking very grubby and dirty mrs roberts his mum looked at him open mouthed just look at the state youre in what you been up to well me and ruth was climbing the wall when i fell off of it replied carlo i ran home quick to tell you mrs roberts looked at carlo you think im gonna believe that go and wash and get changed she ordered its not fair carlo muttered i aint done nothing wrong youre always picking on me

2. Now rewrite the passage, using Standard English.

Sentences (double negatives; subject and verb agreement)

Two common grammatical mistakes are:
- writing sentences which contain **double negatives**
- writing sentences in which **the subject and the verb do not agree**

The boy **did not** have **no** bow.

should be

The boy **did not** have **a** bow.

The arrows **was** in the quiver.

should be

The arrows **were** in the quiver.

A **negative** is a word, or part of a word, that means **no**.

If the **subject** of the sentence is **plural**, the **verb** must also be **plural**.

Practice

Here are some common negatives.

| no | not | nothing | never | nowhere | n't |

Underline the negative words in each of these incorrectly written sentences. Rewrite each sentence correctly.

1. There isn't no point in going out because it's raining.

2. The referee said that he didn't want no trouble.

3. The burglar claimed that he wasn't nowhere near the house when it was burgled.

4. I don't belong to no swimming club.

5. The crocodile hasn't got no whiskers.

6. The toy robot didn't do nothing when I wound it up.

7. The witness said that she never saw nobody.

8. Ranjit would never try nothing new.

9. We haven't got no bananas.

10. I never went nowhere yesterday.

Making sure

These words always take a singular verb:

each	every	one	someone	somebody	anyone	anybody
	everyone	everybody	nobody	no one	none	

Complete these sentences, using the correct form of the verb in brackets.

1. There (was/were) many feathers in his headdress.

2. Here (is/are) the winning Lottery numbers.

3. None of the dogs (was/were) hungry.

4. Emma (isn't/aren't) coming to art club today.

5. (Do/does) anyone know Tom's address?

6. Jamal (did/done) his work before he watched television.

7. It (don't/doesn't) look a very nice day.

8. Every present (was/were) carefully wrapped.

9. Hannah and James (wasn't/ weren't) playing on the computer.

10. All children (have/has) to go to school.

11. Each of the children (was/were) telling the truth.

12. The teacher (give/gave) a spelling test.

Practise your punctuation

Write this passage correctly, putting in the punctuation marks.

robert who was smiling like a cat with the cheese opened the door and shouted mum guess what i done really well in the test at school today thats nice his mum replied what were the test you did it were a spelling test three of us what done well was allowed to go out to play early its a pity i haven't got no sweets or else i would have give you some for trying so hard his mum said my friend jamie didn't get none right robert said as he made himself a jam sandwich

Nouns (gender)

Nouns may be classified according to their **gender**.
A noun may be **masculine**, **feminine**, **common** or **neuter**.

| boy | girl | teacher | desk |

This is a **masculine** (male) noun.

This is a **feminine** (female) noun.

This is a **common** noun. It could refer to a male or a female.

This is a **neuter** noun. **Neuter** means **without gender**.

Practice

1. Match the masculine nouns to the feminine nouns. Write them in pairs.
   The first one has been done for you.

| *Masculine nouns* | boy   father   uncle   son   nephew   king   prince   bridegroom   man   husband   brother |

| *Feminine nouns* | aunt   queen   girl   wife   daughter   mother   woman   niece   princess   bride   sister |

boy ⟶ girl

2. Rewrite these sentences. Change all the masculine nouns into feminine nouns.
   a) My father was talking to my uncle.
   b) The bridegroom smiled at the man who was taking the photographs.
   c) The king was not pleased with his son, the prince.
   d) The eldest brother was going to be the king.

Making sure

1. Copy the chart and write each noun in the correct column.

Masculine	Feminine	Common	Neuter

nun   pupil   tap   secretary   doctor   monk   friend
hotel   policewoman   grandmother   wizard   stepmother
bachelor   earl   cousin   rocket

2. Write the answers to these clues. Write **m** after each masculine noun, **f** after each feminine noun, **c** after each common noun and **n** after each neuter noun. The first one has been done for you.

a) The son of a queen   prince   **m**
b) A woman who is getting married
c) A child whose parents have died
d) A bat used in tennis
e) Someone who writes books
f) A person being treated by a doctor
g) Your uncle's son
h) A person who looks after your teeth

Practise your punctuation

1. Punctuate these sentences correctly.
   a) hissing angrily the snake slithered towards the child
   b) the duke and duchess of windsor attended the theatre to see a play by william shakespeare
   c) what sort of soup is this the old man asked the restaurateur its tomato soup sir she replied
   d) the tongue tied boy who was blushing nervously plucked up courage to ask the girl for a dance
   e) the doctor examined the patient and said i think its just a bad cold you should be better in a few days

2. Now underline all the nouns in the sentences you have written. Write **m** above each masculine noun, **f** above each feminine noun, **c** above each common noun and **n** above each neuter noun.

Shortening and Extending Sentences

The **camels** crossed the **desert**.

> We can **shorten** this sentence by changing the **nouns** into **pronouns**.

They crossed **it**.

> We can **extend** the sentence by adding some **adjectives**.

The **tired**, **dusty** camels crossed the **hot**, **sandy** desert.

> We can **extend** this sentence by adding an **adverb**.

The tired, dusty camels **slowly** crossed the hot, sandy desert.

Practice

1. Shorten these sentences. First, take out all the adjectives and adverbs. Then change the nouns into pronouns. The first one has been done for you.
   a) The fierce dog angrily chased the frightened boy.
      The dog chased the boy. It chased him.
   b) The suntanned girl really enjoyed swimming.
   c) The chattering monkeys noisily climbed the dangling creepers.
   d) My best friend and I ran quickly to the shop.
   e) The handsome, dashing prince swiftly mounted his prancing white stallion.
   f) The glamorous female tennis star eagerly telephoned her new boyfriend.

2. Extend these sentences. Add some adjectives to the nouns. Add an adverb to the verb in each sentence. The first one has been done for you.
   a) The elephant lumbered through the jungle.
      The big, grey elephant lumbered slowly through the hot, steamy jungle.
   b) The man ordered a pizza.
   c) A princess sang a song.
   d) The film was showing at the cinema.
   e) The car spun off the road.
   f) The girl read the book.

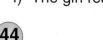

Making sure

1. We can extend a sentence by adding a phrase or a clause. (Look back at Units 5 and 12 to check that you know what phrases and clauses are.)
   Extend each of these sentences with a phrase from the box.
   The first one has been done for you.

   > during the night   with red and white stripes
   > an enormous, gas-filled monstrosity   very soft and squashy
   > a great tower of a man   early in the morning

   a) The tired, dusty camels crossed the hot, sandy desert.
      Early in the morning, the tired, dusty camels crossed the hot, sandy desert.
   b) The hot air balloon floated over the countryside.
   c) The spectators threw rotten tomatoes at the actors.
   d) The sun umbrella blew into the sea.
   e) The giant strode towards the castle.
   f) The owl went out hunting.

2. Extend each of these sentences by adding a clause.
   The first one has been done for you.
   a) The tired, dusty camels crossed the hot, sandy desert.
      The tired, dusty camels crossed the hot, sandy desert and rested at a cool oasis.
   b) The bright sun beat down mercilessly on the desert as _____.
   c) The panda quietly chewed the bamboo shoot and _____.
   d) The mountaineer tried to climb down the steep cliff but _____.
   e) The team was really fed up because _____.
   f) We will never be able to reach the cabin unless _____.

Practise your punctuation

Punctuate this passage correctly.

the strong easterly wind made the sails of the pirate ship billow the ship an old merchant galleon captured long ago was sailing to the caribbean look lively snarled carbuncle cutlass the captain or youll feel the lick of my whip on your backs the crew a ferocious band of cutthroats struggled and sweated as they climbed the rigging cursing the captain silently under their breaths land ahoy came the cry from the crows nest everyone strained their eyes against the sun to see the faint outline of the mysterious island ahead

Progress Test B

1. Add a **prefix** (**im** or **in**) to each of these **adjectives** to give it the opposite meaning.

a) _____ patient   b) _____ visible   c) _____ expensive
d) _____ perfect   e) _____ pure   f) _____ sane

2. Now write a sentence containing each of the **adjectives** you formed in Question1.

3. These **adjectives** have all been made from nouns by the addition of a **suffix**.
   Write the noun from which each **adjective** comes.
   The first one has been done for you.
   a) careful ⟶ care
   b) circular   c) woollen   d) friendly
   e) beautiful   f) golden   g) graceful
   h) wintry   i) muscular   j) cowardly

4. Underline the **main clause** in each sentence. Circle the **subordinate clause**.
   a) The dog chased the postman because it thought he was a burglar.
   b) The greedy girl ate all the sweets before the others got home.
   c) After I had eaten my meal, I brushed my teeth.
   d) I opened the door when the bell rang.
   e) The old lady was still cold although the sun was shining.

5. Write the **conjunction** in each sentence in Question 4.
   a) _____   b) _____   c) _____   d) _____   e) _____

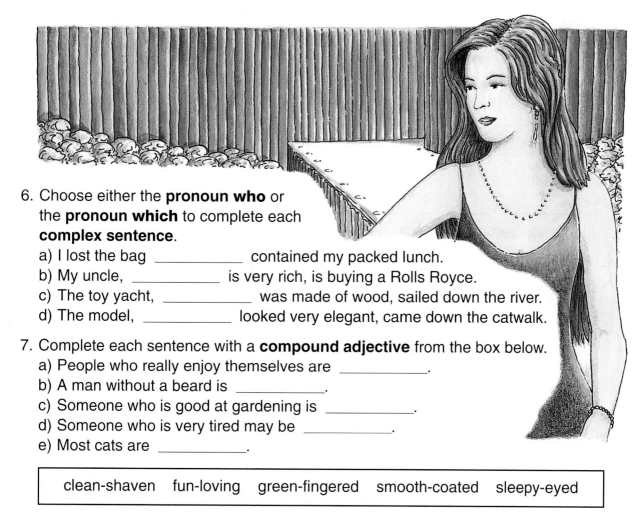

6. Choose either the **pronoun who** or
   the **pronoun which** to complete each
   complex sentence.
   a) I lost the bag _____ contained my packed lunch.
   b) My uncle, _____ is very rich, is buying a Rolls Royce.
   c) The toy yacht, _____ was made of wood, sailed down the river.
   d) The model, _____ looked very elegant, came down the catwalk.

7. Complete each sentence with a **compound adjective** from the box below.
   a) People who really enjoy themselves are _____.
   b) A man without a beard is _____.
   c) Someone who is good at gardening is _____.
   d) Someone who is very tired may be _____.
   e) Most cats are _____.

   | clean-shaven   fun-loving   green-fingered   smooth-coated   sleepy-eyed |

8. Write the **possessive** form of each of these. The first one has been done for you.
   a) the claws of the cat — *the cat's claws*
   b) the apron belonging to the chef
   c) the car belonging to the thieves
   d) the hats of the soldiers
   e) the coat belonging to Mr Bristow
   f) the headlights of the cars

9. Rewrite the following incorrectly written sentences in **Standard English**.
   Look out for **double negatives** and nouns which do not **agree** with verbs.
   a) The girl said, "I aint done nothing wrong."
   b) Tom said he didn't want no sweets.
   c) Mrs Cook never saw nobody she knew in town.
   d) I haven't been nowhere near the wet paint.
   e) Neither Jane nor Marsha were late.
   f) My teacher give me some homework yesterday.
   g) My dad done the crossword easy.
   i) Each of the apples were round and red.
   j) The boys was fighting.

10. Copy the chart. Write each **noun** in the correct column according to its **gender**.

Masculine	Feminine	Common	Neuter

son   aunt   paper   lollipop   tourist   zebra   bus conductor
husband   cup   niece   bride   child

11. Match these sentence beginnings and endings. Write each sentence correctly.

a) An adverb of time

is the name of a thought, idea or feeling.

b) An adjective phrase

contains at least one main clause and one or more subordinate clauses.

c) An abstract noun

tells us when an action took place.

d) A transitive verb

is the form of English usually used in writing.

e) A suffix

is any verb that can take an object.

f) A complex sentence

is a small group of words without a verb that tells us more about a noun.

g) Standard English

may be masculine, feminine, common or neuter.

h) The gender of a noun

is a group of letters we can add to the end of a word to change its meaning.